Book

Science

AR
2.7

1/2/03

First published by Hodder Wayland
338 Euston Road, London NW1 3BH, United Kingdom
Hodder Wayland is an imprint of Hodder Children's
Books, a division of Hodder Headline Limited.
This edition published under license from Hodder
Children's Books. All rights reserved.

Series concept and design by Liz Black
Book design by Jane Hawkins
Edited by Katie Orchard
Science consultant: Dr. Carol Ballard

Published in the United States by
Smart Apple Media
1980 Lookout Drive
North Mankato, Minnesota 56003

Library of Congress Cataloging-in-Publication Data

Godwin, Sam.
All kinds of everything / by Sam Godwin. p. cm. – (Little bees)
Summary: Introduces various types of materials and their
different properties.
1. Materials – Juvenile literature. [1. Materials.]
I. Title.
II. Series.

ISBN 1-58340-251-9

TA403.2 .G63 2002   620.1'1 – dc21   2002023145

9 8 7 6 5 4 3 2 1

All Kinds of Everything

A first look at materials

All Kinds of Everything
A first look at materials

Sam Godwin

A⁺

Smart Apple Media

Everything around us is

Ow! I didn't see that coming!

It's made of glass, Titch. You can see through it, but it's a solid material.

6

made of different materials.

Hey, this window's open! Let's go in.

7

Materials can be solid or liquid.

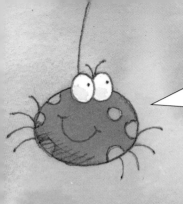

Jello is made from powder or from stretchy cubes.

Hey, Zip, can you stretch everything like jello cubes?

No, Titch. Some hard materials, like glass, can't stretch.

There are hard solids and soft ones.

Liquids flow freely, like water.

13

You can pour liquids into some solid objects.

My tummy can hold a lot of liquid. If only I can get to it!

Zip, could this paper bag hold water?

No, some materials, like paper, aren't waterproof.

Materials change when they become hot.

17

Some solids, like jello cubes, dissolve in water.

Now, where's that chocolate?

Stirring helps the jello to dissolve.

Why is the lady using the wooden spoon instead of the shiny one?

20

Liquids turn into solids when they become cold.

It takes all kinds of materials to make up the world.

Wow! It looks like all those materials have turned into a party!

All about materials

We use lots of different materials every day, such as wood, paper, metal, plastic, glass, sand, stone, wool, and cloth.

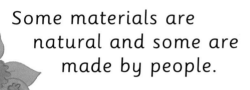

Some materials are natural and some are made by people.

Solids can be hard or soft.

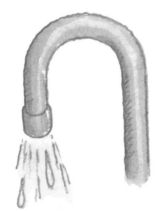

Materials can be solid or liquid.

You can pour some liquids into some solid objects.

Some materials melt when they become hot.

Liquids freeze when they become cold.

The shape of some materials can be changed by bending, twisting, squashing, or stretching them.

Useful Words

Dissolve
When a solid, such as sugar, disappears into a liquid, such as water.

Freeze
When a liquid becomes so cold it turns into a solid. Water becomes ice when it freezes.

Melt
When a solid, such as jello, is heated and turns into a liquid.

Transparent
See-through.

You will see lots of different types of materials at home or at school. Find out which of them are:

warm   squishy   shiny   cold

stretchy   transparent   magnetic

hard   bendy   wobbly   rough

twisty   smooth   bendy   soft

able to float   hot   dull

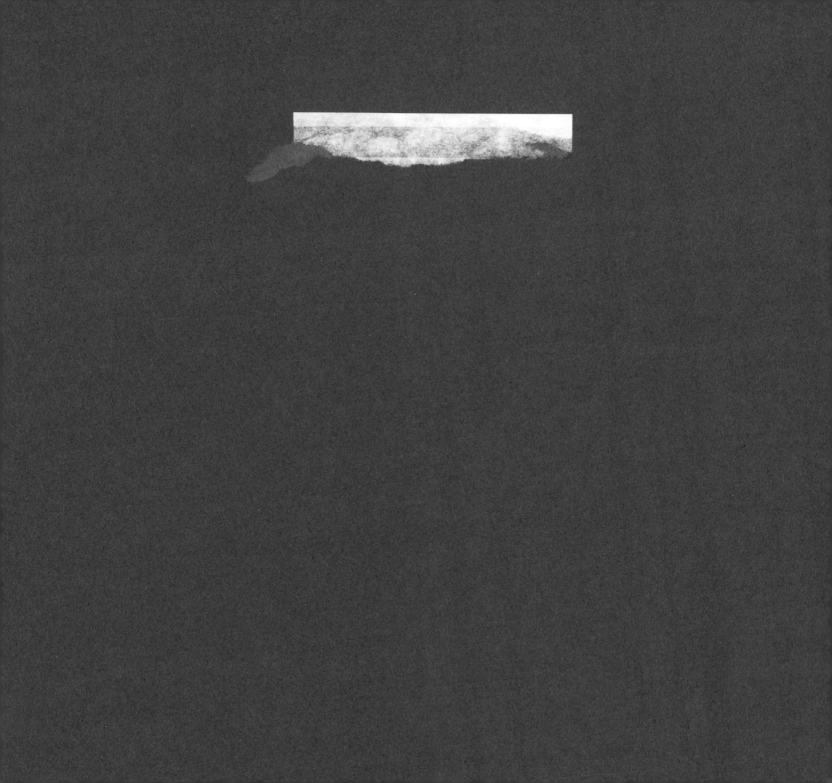